NATIONAL GEOGRAPHIC KiDS

Thank you cards

NATIONAL GEOGRAPHIC
WASHINGTON, D.C.

Designed by Julide Dengel and Spoolia Design
Art direction by Julide Dengel

Text by Girl Friday Productions

ISBN: 978-1-4263-2769-8

Printed in China
17/RRDS/1

Photo Credits
Abbreviations: DRMS-Dreamstime; GI-Getty Images; MP-Minden Pictures; SS-Shutterstock; Cover (Dogs), Mitsuaki Iwago/MP/GI; (Panda), Eric Isselee/SS; (Cheetah), Anup Shah/MP; (Koalas), Eric Isselee/SS; (Lambs), Studio 37/SS; (Sifaka), Konrad Wothe/MP/GI; 1, Eric Isselee/SS; 2, Frank Krahmer/GI; 3 (UP LE), Cyril Ruoso/MP; 3 (UP RT), John Alves/GI; (LO), RGB Ventures/SuperStock/Alamy; 5 (LE), Eric Isselee/SS; 6 (LE), Dima Sidelnikov/SS; (RT), Mandy Godbehear/SS; 7 (LE), Samuel Borges Photography/SS; (RT), Mahathir Mohd Yasin/SS; 8 (UP RT), Courtesy City of London; (LO RT), Alexander Potapov/DRMS; (LO LE), UIG via GI; (UP LE), chuyuss/SS; 9 (UP), Library of Congress; (UP RT), Trinacria Photo/SS; (CTR RT), Image by Mark Avino/National Air and Space Museum/Smithsonian Institution; (LO LE), Eric Isselee/SS; (CTR LE), The Stapleton Collection/Bridgeman Images; (LO RT), Morteza Safataj/SS; 10 (CTR LE), Calvin Chan/SS; (LO), Helmut Corneli/Alamy; 11 (UP), mary416/SS; (CTR), UIG via GI; (LO), Jay Ondreicka/SS; 12-13, Pete Oxford/MP; 17 (RT), Eric Isselee/SS; 18, Zoological Society of San Diego; 19 (UP), Colin Marshall/FLPA/MP; (CTR), Artush/GI; (LO), Anup Shah/NPL/MP; 20 (UP), kim7/SS; (LO), Alan Jeffery/SS; 21 (UP LE), Lightpoet/SS; (UP RT), Lightpoet/SS; (CTR), Stephen Frink/Digital Vision; (LO LE), Brianguest/DRMS; 22-23, Simon Litten/FLPA MP; 24, Marcel Jancovic/SS; 25 (UP), Amaviael/DRMS; (CTR), Maljalen/SS; (LO), Jovanka Novakovic/iStockphoto/GI; 26 (UP RT), AP Photo/Elaine Thompson; (LO RT), Zuzule/SS; (LO LE), cs333/SS; (UP LE), Fotokostic/SS; 27 (UP), Science Source/GI; (CTR RT), vkilikov/SS; (CTR), Courtesy Marine Corp; (LO LE), Paul J. Richards/AFP/GI; (LO CTR), GI; 28 (LE), Katherine Feng/MP; (RT), Dale A Stork/SS; 29, Sevenke/SS; 30 (LE), Louisanne/SS; (RT), Eric Isselee/SS; 31 (UP LE), Rawpixel.com/SS; (CTR UP), Veronica Louro/SS; (CTR), ZouZou/SS; (CTR LO), Monkey Business Images/SS; 32, Eric Isselee/SS; Postcards: (Bears), Barrett Hedges/National Geographic RF/GI; (Cheetah), Anup Shah/MP; (Koalas), Mitsuaki Iwago/MP; (Dolphins), Konrad Wothe/MP; (Donkeys), Blue Iris/SS; (Ducklings), Remco van Daalen/NiS/MP; (Dog-Horse), Ksenia Raikova/iStockphoto/GI; (Red Panda), Qiming Yao/DRMS; (Giraffe), Cyril Ruoso/MP; (Mouse), Klein and Hubert/MP; (Elephants), Javarman/SS; (Kittens-Dog), Ermolaev Alexander/SS; (Lion), Beverly Joubert/National Geographic Creative; (Manatees), James R.D. Scott/GI; (Meerkats), EcoPrint/SS; (Dogs), Hramovnick/iStockphoto/GI; (Owls), Tania Thomson/SS; (Penguins), Jan Vermeer/MP; (Pigs), talseN/SS; (Polar Bear), Steven Kazlowski/NPL/MP; (Rhino), Pete Oxford/NPL/MP; (Sea Otters), Frans Lanting/National Geographic Creative; (Gecko), Piotr Naskrecki/MP; (Turtle), David Carbo/SS; (Spider), Herman Wong HM/SS; (Wolves), Tim Davis/Corbis/GI; (Squirrel), Andy Trowbridge/SS; (Snake), Daniel Heuclin/NPL/MP; (Sheep), Baronb/SS; (Frog), Vince Burton/NiS/MP; Back Cover (Bears), Barrett Hedges/National Geographic RF/GI; (Pigs), talseN/SS; (Meerkat), Aaron Amat/SS; Spine, Aaron Amat/SS

Thank you for saying THANK YOU!

Thanks for being the coolest!

Thanks for having my back!

Thanks for being otter-ly awesome!

Have you ever thought about how many times a day you say "thank you"?

Being thankful and expressing gratitude is all part of human nature. It makes it easier to get along with others, and—let's face it—it's the polite thing to do. You've probably already got it down pat.

But saying "thank you" is just the beginning. Did you know that there's so much more behind it? So much **science, history, even culture?** It's not just humans who do it—your furry friends do, too!

In *National Geographic Kids Thank You Cards*, you'll discover all kinds of ways to show your friends and family that you appreciate them ... and you'll discover you're not alone in your attitude of gratitude! These pages are jam-packed with **fun facts and true tales** about how creatures of all shapes and sizes give each other a pat on the back! So if you'd be so kind as to turn the page ...
Thank you very much!

You deserve a round of applause!

BECOMING A GRATITUDE GURU

You hear people say it all the time: "Thanks!" And being thankful is something people have been practicing and studying for thousands of years.

By now, you've probably said "thank you" thousands—or tens of thosands!—of times in your life. Maybe you even know how to thank people in more than one language. And it probably seems super simple, right? Someone passes the salt and you say thanks; you get a gift and you send a thank-you; someone gives you a compliment and you give them thanks right back. But do you know why you say thank you so much?

Being thankful is a huge part of being polite, of course. But it's also a **building block of human history.** People have been giving thanks for thousands of years, from showing gratitude for bountiful harvests to thanking neighboring kingdoms. Practicing gratitude has allowed different societies to communicate and form alliances, and to share new technologies, food, and innovations.

Thankfulness continues to shape society today. You have likely never thought of saying thanks as part of who you are, but how you show gratitude is probably completely different from the ways kids in other countries give thanks. They may even celebrate different holidays devoted to being grateful.

And get this—**scientists are still learning the secrets of saying thanks.** Expressing gratitude can affect your mood, relationships—even your brain.

So if you think you know everything there is to know about saying thanks, think again—and get ready to learn the secrets of gratitude that will **make you an expert at thank-yous!**

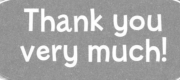

Thank you very much!

Thank you for being awesome!

MERCI!

Thanks for always being there for me!

DANKE!

Thanks a bunch!

Thanks for the cool gift!

Thanks for all your help!

GRACIAS!

Thanks for everything!

Why Say "Thanks"?

Not only does gratitude make other people happy, it also **does great things** for your brain and body. Feeling thankful activates areas of the brain that help you sleep better, lower your stress, and better understand someone else's point of view. It also releases chemicals like dopamine and oxytocin, which give us feelings of joy. That's a recipe for happiness! Scientists say that practicing gratitude is like training a gratitude muscle. Just like when you play sports or exercise, you will get better at it the more you do it. So try these tips to become an all-star gratitude athlete!

Before you go to bed each night, **think of three things** that made you grateful during the day.

Spread the joy— try thanking your friends and family for the **little things they do** that make you happy.

Mastering Mindfulness

You can feel how gratitude helps your body even as it's happening. Here's a mindful way to help you recognize this feeling:

1. Go somewhere quiet, where there are **no distractions**.

2. Sit down in a comfortable position and close your eyes.

3. Take five deep, slow breaths.

4. Check in with your body and mind. How do you feel in this moment? Sadness, happiness, anger, joy, numbness—having any of these or other feelings is perfectly normal.

5. Now, think about something that makes you **feel grateful**. It can be anything—a person, a place, or a thing.

6. Where do you feel it in your body? **How do you feel now?**

REMEMBER: ANY TIME YOU WANT THIS FEELING, ALL YOU HAVE TO DO IS THINK A GRATEFUL THOUGHT!

Create a **gratitude jar.** Decorate a jar or box, and every time you feel grateful, write a little note about it and **place it inside.** Any time you need a gratitude reminder, take the notes out and **read them!**

At dinnertime, ask your family members about the **three best parts of their day.** Then share your own!

Thank yourself! Did you try extra hard at school? Make an effort to do your chores? Maybe go out of your way to help a friend? Recognize your own **awesome actions** and give yourself a pat on the back.

Famous Thank Yous
Throughout History

2000 B.C.

Ancestor veneration in China, a form of honoring, thanking, and enlisting the aid of one's ancestors, is thought to have originated with the Xia dynasty around 2000 B.C.

1421

When London helped finance a winning battle against the French in the Hundred Years' War, King Henry V of England presented the city with a gift of thanks: a priceless scepter made of gold, pearls, and precious jewels.

1350 B.C.

If you think your letters take a long time to write, think again. In ancient Egypt, a thank-you letter sent to Queen Tiye from a neighboring king was carved into clay!

A.D. 250–900

To honor various gods and thank them for their favor, the ancient Maya offered up tributes of thanks. These offerings were often cast into sacred cenotes—natural sinkholes filled with groundwater—and could include pottery, food, or even human sacrifices.

350 B.C.–A.D. 400

In ancient Greece and Rome, many philosophers debated the art of the perfect "thank you." In fact, they believed that when given a gift, the recipient should say thanks by giving back an even better gift—sort of making "thanks" a competition in which the winner was more polite (but the loser got a better gift).

1918

In 1918, to celebrate the end of WWI, U.S. president Woodrow Wilson declared November 11th "Armistice Day." The holiday was renamed **Veterans Day** in 1954, and is dedicated to thanking and honoring the service of all U.S. military veterans.

PRESENT TIME

Founded in 1910, Hallmark is now one of the **largest greeting card companies** in the world; the company recently sold 4,750,000,000 cards in one year.

1873

If you haven't yet warmed up to the idea of sending thank-you notes (don't worry, you will!), try blaming **Louis Prang** for your pains. This Prussian printer, sometimes called the "**Father of the American Christmas Card**," is known for introducing greeting cards to America and England.

MAY YOU HAVE A QUITE TOO HAPPY TIME

1994

If you safely traveled to the moon and back, you'd probably be super-relieved, right? Well, so was **Neil Armstrong**, who sent a heartfelt thank-you letter to the engineering team that designed his **history-making space suit**.

sorry ...

1600

Gratitude is an important part of life to many indigenous Americans. One **Lakota legend**, possibly originating around 1600, tells the story of an **ungrateful bear** who is punished for not recognizing the aid of a family of kind badgers.

1945

Talk about the gift that keeps on giving: In 1945, the grateful Dutch royal family sent **100,000 tulip bulbs** to Canada as a thank-you for its aid during WWII. These days, Canada hosts an annual **tulip festival**, which draws more than 500,000 visitors a year.

9

A World of Thanks

How do you give thanks? Do you send a letter after getting a gift or chow down on turkey during Thanksgiving? Or maybe you eat mooncakes, participate in a traditional dance, or join a parade? That's the beauty of thank-yous—there are so many ways to say them! Take a peek at how people express gratitude across the globe.

Thaipusam (TIE-poos-am)

Thaipusam is a big festival of thanks and penance, or making up for something you've done wrong, for Hindus all over the world. For a month beforehand, devotees maintain a strict vegetarian diet to spiritually prepare themselves. The occasion is marked by a colorful procession to the temple, where devotees leave offerings and receive sacred ash.

Dating back more than **4,000** years, Hinduism is mainly practiced in India. There are over 950 million Hindus worldwide.

Erntedankfest
(airn-t-DAHNK-fest)

Though this is not an official holiday in Germany, many people in this part of the world celebrate **Erntedankfest** (harvest festival of thanks) in the fall. After a church service, people join together to walk in a thanksgiving procession, at the end of which a harvest crown is presented to the harvest queen.

Traditionally, Germans ate **chicken** or **rooster** for this holiday meal, but these days some folks have adopted the American tradition of eating turkey, too.

Moon Festival

China's Moon Festival is an ancient tradition in which people worshipped the moon goddess, Chang'e, and gave their thanks for the harvest. On the autumn night that has the brightest full moon, friends and family eat mooncakes (a flaky pastry), light lanterns, and burn incense.

The Moon Festival is also celebrated in **Malaysia, Vietnam, Singapore,** and **Korea.** In Vietnam, it is sometimes called "Children's Festival" because it celebrates children. Parents cook their kids' favorite meals and even buy them toys!

Homowo
(ho-MO-wo)

Homowo is celebrated by the Ga people of Ghana, to remember times of famine and to celebrate the return of the rains. For this holiday, they take a break from work to stage parades, beat drums, paint their faces, sing songs of praise, and perform traditional dances—all as thanks for their good fortune.

The Plymouth Pilgrims celebrated the first Thanksgiving in **1621.** The **Wampanoag Indians**— who had taught the Pilgrims how to cultivate the land—were invited to the feast.

Thanksgiving

In the United States, **Thanksgiving** is a day for friends and family to gather for a big meal (and sometimes to watch football). Many people enjoy saying grace, a sort of prayer, or giving thanks around the table.

Thank you for the doggone good food!

Thanks A TON!

What are whale sharks grateful for? Food—and plenty of it! These gentle giants are filter feeders and spend their time snacking on plankton, krill, and other small fish in warm and tropical waters.

Whale sharks are the **largest fish in the sea.**

Whale sharks can weigh **up to 11 tons (10 t).**

August 30th is **International Whale Shark Day.**

It's Your Turn!
Flex Those Gratitude Muscles!

Want to be the greatest at gratitude? Peerless at praise? The all-star of appreciation? Then get to training! Take a moment to think of the things that make you want to say "thanks." By taking this time to focus on being thankful, you'll strengthen the areas of your brain that respond to gratitude. You'll also improve your health and happiness. That's a win-win, all-star!

What are some things you're grateful for?

_____

_____

_____

_____

_____

_____

When was the last time you said thanks?

_____

_____

_____

_____

What is the nicest thing someone has done for you?

_____
_____
_____
_____
_____

What are some things you appreciate about yourself?

_____
_____
_____
_____
_____

What is your favorite way to say thank you?

_____
_____
_____
_____
_____

THE WILD WORLD OF GRATITUDE

So now you're an expert on gratitude in the human world ... but how does it all work in the animal kingdom?

Believe it or not, humans are not the only ones who help each other out. Whether it's a **chimpanzee** grooming the delicious bugs from a relative's back or a **wildebeest** alerting his herd to danger, **animals have endless ways to be caring and kind.** In fact, tons of animals rely on this helpful behavior to find food, avoid predators, stay healthy, and more.

And it's not just animals who benefit from this kindness! From helping us farm to providing transportation to acting as our close companions, **wild and domestic creatures** have been teaching humans important

lessons and helping us lead better lives for thousands of years.

You probably have your own reasons to be thankful for animals, too. Maybe you have a **beloved pet who cheers you up** when you're sad, or maybe you drink milk, eat cheese, or wear clothing made from wool.

Whatever the reason, **it's clear that we owe a lot to animals.** Read on to find out just how our furry friends help out each other—and us. You'll even discover more ways to develop your newly trained gratitude muscles, and give back to the kind creatures who deserve our thanks.

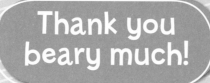

Amazing Animal Teamwork

Just like you might help out a friend or a family member, many animals depend on each other to lend a helping hand—er, paw. And it's not just members of the same species that work together—read on to find out about a lot of different animals who are likely grateful for each other's company.

I'm thankful for our friendship!

No kitten!

Best Friends

Zoos are wonderful places to see animals make friends—including some that would definitely not buddy up had they met face-to-face in the wild. The San Diego Zoo has raised cheetah kittens and dog puppies together. Not only do they play and cuddle, but the dogs also help teach the fierce cats some zoo-friendly social cues. Inspired by the zoo's success, other zoos have started to do this, too.

Dogs pant up to 300 times a minute.

Hold On Tight

If you take a ride on a crab's back, is it still a "piggyback"? Sea anemones might not care about the answer to that riddle, but they do love to hitch a ride on the shells of hermit crabs. It's a fair trade: During the trip, anemones provide camouflage for their crabby chauffeurs while picking up scraps on the ocean floor.

When a hermit crab **starts to outgrow** its shell, it searches for a vacant one.

Safety First

Out on the African savanna, **wherever you find zebras, you'll often also find ostriches.** This is because zebras have poor eyesight, and ostriches have poor senses of hearing and smell. But, by combining their abilities, they cover for one another—zebras listen and smell for the ostriches' predators, and ostriches keep a lookout for the zebras'!

Ostrich nurseries have as many as **300** chicks.

Dinner's on Me

Warthogs use their big strong tusks for defense. But they have no need to defend themselves against mongooses—warthogs let mongooses crawl all over their bodies to remove their ticks. In exchange, the mongoose gets a snack! Not what we'd call a gourmet meal, but the mongooses sure seem to enjoy it.

A warthog's **"warts"** actually serve a purpose: During mating seasons, the male warthogs fight, and these fleshy pads provide cushion for the blows.

19

Righteous Roomies

Think back—have you ever had to share your space with a sibling, relative, or even a friend? They might have been annoying at times, but you probably came together to help out with chores, play games, or tackle homework. Well, like humans, many animals share their spaces with "roommates" of their own. And while they may not have chore charts, they do band together to help each other thrive. Check out these amazing animal roommates!

Cool Colonies

Ant colonies are made up of thousands of ants, each with a designated role. Most of the ants are female workers who spend their time building and maintaining their shared home—the anthill—and searching for leaves and dead insects to eat. The other females are soldiers, who defend the colony as well as occasionally attack other rival colonies. There are usually only one or two queen ants—her job is to mate with the few males and then lay eggs.

Ants can carry up to **20 times** their own body weight!

We're howl-ways better as a team!

Perfect Packs

Wolves live together in groups called packs. Usually led by an alpha male and female couple, the group can include up to 15 wolves. It has a complex social order, made up of the alphas, their young, and other adult wolves that don't have pups of their own. It's only by working together as a team that they can bring down animals much larger than themselves, such as moose or bison.

Thanks for bee-ing a hard worker!

Hardworking Hives

Honeybees live together in a hive, an ingenious honeycomb structure made out of wax. There can be up to 35,000 bees in a single hive! Much like ants, bees have certain roles: female workers, male drones (whose only job is to breed with the queen), and one big queen who lays all the eggs. Worker bees collect pollen and nectar from plants to make their food source: honey, that sweet treat that other organisms, like humans and bears, love to eat.

Super Schools

Though it may look like a **school of fish** is playing "follow the leader," in reality there is no leader. Rather, these yellowtailed surgeonfish synchronize their movements by sight and by using a special sense that feels movement in the water. Most scientists agree that fish form schools because there is "safety in numbers"—the glint and glimmer of a school's scales can confuse predators.

A school of fish is known as a "troubling."

Great Gaggles

Have you ever seen a **gaggle of geese** flying in a V shape? They don't do this just because it looks cool! It's for efficiency: The geese up front help reduce the air resistance for those behind them. And because it's hard work, the geese take turns by switching places when they get tired. Those in the rear honk their encouragement to the leaders.

When a goose is injured, often a **fellow goose** will stay with it until it rejoins the gaggle.

A hare can run at **35 miles an hour (56 km/h).**

Rabbits have almost **twice as many taste buds** on their tongues as humans.

A rabbit's teeth **grow its entire life.**

Wild rabbits need speed and agility to survive, so they are probably thankful for their powerful legs and sharp hearing. For pet bunnies, it's another story entirely! These domestic fluffballs are likely most grateful for gentle pats and great chow.

Doggone Thankful

If you have a dog, you probably already know why they are considered human's best friend. But canines are highly intelligent animals who can do a lot more than just beg for treats or curl up next to you on the couch when you're watching TV. Here are some cool and courageous ways these fabulous pets help us humans.

Getting There

Before the snowmobile, **sled dogs** were essential helpers for humans living in Arctic regions around the world. Bred to withstand freezing temperatures and treacherous terrain, they worked hauling people and supplies across the ice. Today, the Iditarod, a nearly **1,200-mile (1,931-km) race across** Alaska, celebrates dog sledding, and attracts mushers and their sled dogs for this serious—and seriously cold—sport. **Brrrrr!**

Sled dogs can run up to 20 miles an hour (32 km/h).

Thanks for leading the pack!

On the Job

From airports to war zones, bomb-sniffing dogs work hard to stop disaster before it strikes. Trained to use their extraordinary noses to **sniff out the chemicals** used in bombs, they alert their handlers by wagging their tails briskly and pulling on the leash. **These brave canines save lives!**

Dogs smell in layers, so they can detect bomb-building materials even if they are masked by another odor.

Friends Forever

Whether you're hanging out with a 12-pound (5-kg) Chihuahua or a 110-pound (50-kg) Bernese mountain dog, humans often form close social bonds with their furry friends. Dogs were domesticated as pets thousands of years ago. So for a very long time, their job has been to love, love, and love. The Humane Society estimates that almost half of the households in the United States have a dog!

Some scientists think that as gray wolves started hanging around **human campfires** thousands of years ago, they became tamer on their own, instead of being tamed by humans.

A Helping Paw

Service dogs work to help people with disabilities in many different kinds of ways. Depending on the person in their care, their duties include alerting their person to sound, pulling wheelchairs, reminding someone to take her medication, picking up dropped items, standing guard, or going for help.

Golden retrievers, sometimes nicknamed "**goldens**," are highly intelligent and frequently used as guide dogs for the blind.

Animals That Lent a Helping Hoof

Courageous canines, hardworking horses, daring dolphins, and brave birds: Meet some of history's awesome animals that deserve your thanks.

3000 B.C.

Though cats had already been employed as mousers for thousands of years, in Egypt **cats are considered sacred and mummified as part of religious rituals.**

20,000–10,000 B.C.

Originally **wolves and humans competed for food,** but over time their close proximity allowed some wolves to become domesticated, evolving into what are now domestic dogs—*Canis familiaris* (the *familiaris* part of their name comes from the word "familiar"). These early dogs helped protect human settlements and used their wolflike instincts to help humans hunt.

1591

Marocco the Dancing Horse was famous in England for counting coins, dancing on his hind legs, and even bowing to the queen. Rumor had it that he had psychic abilities. Because of this, he and his owner were condemned for witchcraft, but Marocco saved both of their lives by kneeling before the judge.

9000–7000 B.C.

Goats, sheep, cows, and pigs are domesticated for their **meat, dairy, and hides.**

4000 B.C.

Larger animals, such as oxen, water buffalo, and horses, are domesticated for reasons beyond providing food—**they are trained to help with plowing farm fields and to provide transportation.**

1948

A Rhesus monkey named Albert I was the first primate to be launched into space. Though he did not survive the trip, his contribution—along with those of many other primate and dog astronauts—was essential to our continued exploration of space.

2007

In New Zealand, four lifeguards were doing a training swim when a pod of bottlenose dolphins arrived, formed a circle, and began to herd them. At first the lifeguards were confused—until they saw the great white shark swimming nearby. The dolphins had come to escort them to safety.

1952

A mare named Reckless served in the U.S. Marine Corps during the Korean War. Her job was to deliver ammunition to the field and to help evacuate wounded soldiers. She was promoted to staff sergeant and received many awards for bravery, including two Purple Hearts.

1918

During World War I, carrier pigeon Cher Ami delivered a message from a lost battalion of the 77th Infantry Division to the U.S. Army Signal Corps that identified their location in the French countryside. Because of his job well done, over 200 soldiers were saved.

1996

Dolly the sheep—the first cloned mammal—was "born." Technically known as "6LL3," this successful experiment is considered one of the most significant breakthroughs in science.

Thanking Our Furry Friends

With all that Earth's creatures do for us, how exactly can we repay the kindness? Animals are our friends and neighbors around the world, but habitat loss, hunting, and other human activities threaten countless species. Luckily, there are many people around the world who are trying to make the world a better place for us and our four-legged friends, and you can help! It's time to express your gratitude—animal-style.

Rockin' Rescues

Animal rescue shelters take in neglected, abused, or abandoned domestic animals, like dogs and cats. There the animals receive medical care, food, and love. The main mission of these shelters is to match their temporary residents with humans looking to adopt a pet so that together they can make a forever home.

There are an estimated **10,000** rescue groups and animal shelters in North America.

Pawsome Preserves

A wildlife preserve is a designated territory in which animals and the land are protected from human threats. The rangers and other staff at a preserve work to ensure that poachers or loggers do not injure animals or the habitat. Special preserves in China are working to help the vulnerable giant panda by raising cubs and releasing them onto protected land.

Super Sanctuaries

A wildlife sanctuary is a place for wildlife who have been injured or for some reason can't return to the wild. The animals within a sanctuary are cared for by humans while they live in a habitat that is as close to the habitat they are from as possible. Some wildlife sanctuaries in the United States include elephant sanctuaries for elephants that once lived in zoos or circuses.

Ways to Be Involved in Helping Animals

Raise money through a bake sale or talent show and give the proceeds to an animal-related charity.

If you are getting a new pet, **suggest that your family adopt** from your local humane society. Your new buddy will appreciate your loving home!

Adopt a wild animal. No, we're not suggesting you bring a Komodo dragon or Tasmanian devil home. Instead, families can give money to a trusted organization to support an endangered animal.

Help your parents to be smart shoppers. Find out whether the products your family buys are safe for animals and the planet.

Educate yourself. Knowledge is power! Join kids.nationalgeographic .com/mission-animal-rescue to stay in the know.

Be a picky eater. Ask your parents if the eggs and meat they buy are humanely raised. If you eat seafood, be sure that it's harvested humanely.

Sign a petition or write a letter to the representatives in your state.

Ways You Can Help

To learn more about what you can do, grab a parent and visit:

1. American Society for the Prevention of Cruelty to Animals (www.aspca.org)
2. Animal Charities of America (www.animalcharitiesofamerica.org)
3. Endangered Fish Alliance (endangeredfishalliance.org)
4. The Humane Society (www.humanesociety.org)
5. National Geographic (www.nationalgeographic.com) and National Geographic Kids (kids.nationalgeographic.com)
6. National Wildlife Foundation (nwf.org)
7. PAWS (www.paws.org)
8. The World Wildlife Fund (wwf.org)

Don't forget to say thanks!

It's Your Turn!
What Happens When You Say "Thanks!"?

So someone has done something nice for you, and you want to say thank you. Now what? Here are some tips and tricks for manners masters:

If you open a present in front of someone, you can say thank you right then and there, but always follow up with a hand-written card.

If you receive a bunch of presents at once (for your birthday, bar/bat mitzvah, graduation, etc.), write down who gave you what as you open them. This will make it easy to remember who gave you what gift, plus save you a lot of time later on when you write the thank-you cards. Don't forget to thank the party planner, too!

When it comes to writing a thank-you note, the sooner the better. Less than a week after the gesture is best. And the sooner you do it, the sooner you can check it off your to-do list. But it's never too late to send a thank-you card!

If someone gives you money, write in the thank-you card how you're going to use it.

For other gifts, write in the thank-you card how you plan to use the gift, or that you'll think of the gift-giver every time you see their gift.

If you're thanking someone for having you over or doing something nice for you, mention specifics about what you enjoyed or appreciated about it.

So, when would I write an otterly perfect thank you note?

Try writing a note when ...

a friend or family member invites you for a special meal

you have an overnight or longer stay at someone's house

a friend does you a special favor

thanking a teacher or sports coach for their guidance

Check out this example for ideas on how to write an A+ thank-you note:

BE POLITE.
Begin your note with a formal greeting.

Dear Aunt Susan,

EXPRESS YOUR THANKS.

Thank you so much

BE SPECIFIC.
State exactly what you're thanking the person for.

for your generous gift for my graduation.

GET PERSONAL.
Explain how you plan to use the gift or what their gesture meant to you.

My parents suggested that I put half in my savings account. The other half I'm going to use to buy a new chew toy for my dog, Harold. He's going to be so happy!

END WITH A WARM SIGN-OFF.

Many thanks,

Jeremy

Dear Aunt Susan,

Thank you so much for your generous gift for my graduation. My parents suggested that I put half in my savings account. The other half I'm going to use to buy a new chew toy for my dog, Harold. He's going to be so happy!

Many thanks,
Jeremy

It's Your Turn!
Thank You Cards You Can USE

On the following pages, use these awesome thank-you cards to send to friends, family, or anyone who you want to thank in your life.

Directions

1. **Write** your special message on the back.

2. **Fill out** the name and address of your recipient.

3. **Don't forget** to put a stamp on it if you're sending it through the mail.

4. **Deliver** your thank-you card.

Practice your writing skills on the blank card below

Dear_____,

Thank you!

HOW To Say thank you In 50 Different Languages:

AFRIKAANS
DANKIE
(DAHN-kee)

ALBANIAN
FALEMINDERIT
(fah-lehm-meen-DEH-reet)

ARABIC
SHUKRAN
(shoo-krahn)

ARMENIAN
CHNORAKALOUTIOUN
(shno-ra-ka-loo-TYOON)

BOSNIAN
HVALA
(HVAH-lah)

BULGARIAN
BLAGODARIA
(blah-goh-DAH-ryah)

CATALAN
GRÀCIES
(GRAH-syuhs)

CANTONESE
M̀H'GŌI
(M̀h'gōi) (for a service)

CANTONESE
DÒJEH
(dò-jeh) (for a gift)

CROATIAN
HVALA
(HVAH-lah)

CZECH
DĚKUJI
(de-koo-yih)

DANISH
TAK
(tahg)

DUTCH
DANK U
(dahnk yuh)

ESTONIAN
TÄNAN
(TA-nahn)

Thank you BEARY MUCH!

Your help was spot-on! THANKS!

Thank you for being a KOALA-ty friend!

When a bear cub is born, it's no bigger than a chipmunk.

Cheetahs are the fastest land animals, reaching speeds of more than 60 miles an hour (97 km/h).

For most animals, eucalyptus leaves are poisonous. But koalas may eat more than two pounds (1 kg) of them a day!

YOU DOLPHIN-ITELY DESERVE THANKS!

THANKS FOR STICKING BY ME!

THANK YOU FOR LEADING THE WAY!

Dolphins blow bubbles to communicate.

In the United Kingdom, all donkeys are required to have a passport.

Ducklings won't replace their yellow fuzz with adult feathers until they're about two months old.

HOW To Say thank you In 50 Different Languages:

LEBANESE
SHUKRAN
(SHOO-krahn)

LITHUANIAN
AČIŪ
(AH-choo)

MACEDONIAN
БЛАГОДАРАМ
(blah-GOH-dah-rahm)

MALAY
TERIMA KASIH
(TREE-muh KAH-seh)

MALTESE
GRAZZI
(GRUTS-ee)

MANDARIN
谢谢
(shyeh-shyeh)

MONGOLIAN
БАЯРЛАЛАА
(ba-yar-la-laa)

NORWEGIAN
TAKK
(tak)

POLISH
DZIĘKUJĘ
(jen-KOO-yeh)

PORTUGUESE
OBRIGADO [Masculine]
(oh-bree-GAH-doo)

PORTUGUESE
OBRIGADA [Feminine]
(oh-bree-GAH-dah)

ROMANIAN
MULŢUMESC
(mool-tzoo-MESK)

RUSSIAN
СПАСИБО
(spuh-SEE-buh)

SERBIAN
ХВАЛА
(HVAH-lah)

THANKS FOR MAKING MY **RUFF** DAY BETTER!

THANKS FOR BEING THERE FOR ME THROUGH ALL THE **PANDA-MONIUM!**

TWEET

THANKS FOR ALWAYS STICKING **YOUR NECK** OUT FOR ME!

Dogs can see yellow, blue, and violet. Horses can only see blue and green.

Red pandas are more closely related to skunks than to black-and-white giant pandas.

An adult male giraffe can grow up to 18 feet (5.5 m)—taller than three adult humans.

THANKS FOR HELPING ME REACH NEW HEIGHTS!

I HERD YOU WERE GREAT ... BUT YOU REALLY LEAD THE WAY!

THANKS FOR BEING TOTALLY PAWESOME.

YOU'RE THE CAT'S MEOW!

A mouse's tail can grow to be the same length as its body.

_____
_____
_____
_____

When elephants swim in deep water, they use their trunks like snorkels.

_____
_____
_____
_____

Some dogs are allergic to cats!

_____
_____
_____
_____